NAVIGATING THE SOCIAL SECURITY DISABILITY MAZE

Written Exclusively for Disability Applicants

First Edition

JUDGE RONALD A. MARKS

GOLDEN ORIOLE PUBLISHING, LTD.
Hubbard, Ohio

Published by

Golden Oriole Publishing, Ltd.
Hubbard, Ohio

ISBN: 0615590462
ISBN 13: 9780615590462

Jacket Design: Paul Ferrara. New York, New York

To my wife

Elaine Marks

The opinions expressed here are based on my experience, interaction with my colleagues, observations of claimants in the courtroom and listening to Medical and Vocational Experts. These opinions are mine and mine alone. Only government documents readily available on the internet were used as background in writing this book. Other sources are my recollection of events of typical claimants and their representatives during hearings.

I do not promise or guarantee that buying this book will get you a favorable decision from Social Security. No lawyer client relationship is intended nor created by your purchase of and reliance on the contents of this book.

INTRODUCTION

When applying for Social Security Disability your credibility will be issue number one from filing the application through the hearing before an Administrative Law Judge. You must be truthful in all things you say and do in order to "Navigate the Social Security Disability Maze."

Credibility once lost is difficult, if not impossible, to get back. Every step of the Social Security Disability process presents an opportunity for you to enhance or solidify your credibility. During my judicial career with the Social Security Administration thousands of regular hard working people appeared before me sick or injured and out of work. They also arrived for their hearings with detailed supportive medical records. They came represented by capable advocates. They were worried about providing for their families. Then, much to my dismay, some of these claimants would exaggerate, be inconsistent about the symptoms and limitations of their illness or injury and testify in a way that was not credible. They tried to fool me and they threw it all away.

This book is not written for lawyers or other professionals but for claimants like yourself. "Navigating…" is not intended as a replacement for what a qualified Social Security representative can do for you. However, much of what I have to offer you is beyond the training and experience of most skilled professionals.

The advice I provide here is what I tell clients in my private practice since retiring from the Social Security Administration. You will benefit from my 30 plus years of Social Security Disability practice and the Social Security Judicial positions

I held at the highest levels of the Social Security Disability program.

Remember, the Judge you appear before will be the final judge of your truthfulness. There may be staff members and even experts at your hearing who form opinions about your credibility. Their opinions, by law, will not count and cannot even be considered. The Judge and no one else will decide your credibility and then must explain his or her decision in writing.

My advice to all those applying for disability? Tell the truth, even if it hurts.

TABLE OF CONTENTS

CHAPTER 1

SHOULD I HIRE SOMEONE TO REPRESENT ME?

As a Social Security Disability applicant you are entitled to be represented at your hearing. If you go to a hearing by yourself the Judge is required to explain your rights on the record and give you a continuance to get representation.

The Judge will tell you that you may be represented by a lawyer or non- lawyer. You may even ask a relative or friend to represent you. No matter who represents you, a form 1696 will have to be filed, giving notice of who that person is. The Judge will also instruct you that no fee may be charged by your representative unless and until she approves it.

Moreover, if you are not able to pay a representative the Judge will explain there are organizations that represent such people if you meet the income/asset qualifications. You may even be given a list of such organizations by a staff member. If after an explanation of your rights and the nature of the proceedings you want a continuance to hire someone the Judge should grant your request. If you return a second time without a representative the Judge will likely deny any requests for a further continuance. Many of my colleagues, including me, will grant a second continuance if you have made significant efforts to find someone. When you return be sure to have evidence of all phone calls to those you contacted and it should help you.

If you have decided to hire someone to represent you read on. If you haven't decided, read on anyway, my observations from the bench should help you decide. With or without a representative you will gain valuable advice from reading "Navigating the Social Security Disability Maze."

Your hesitancy at hiring someone may be well founded. When people turn to the federal government for help it is because they have faith their government exists to help them. This is particularly true with the Social Security Administration and the disability program. Some claimants believe they are entitled to disability checks without going through the entire process.

I just started a hearing in Cleveland early in my career as a Judge when a woman asked that very question. After being seated and taking the oath she said "Your Honor, When do I get my check?" But, of course, it is not that easy. There are due process requirements. Protection of the Social Security Trust Fund is also an issue so the process can be frustrating.

The Social Security disability program is an entitlement program that also requires, at the Administrative Law Judge (ALJ) level, proof of disability. The required proof must be provided by a combination of the documents in the claimant's file including medical records and, of course, claimant's testimony.

Congress created the disability program through legislation and the implementing regulations. The President signed the legislation and the program became law. Drafting of the specific regulations for the Social Security Disability program was delegated to the Commissioner of Social Security. But it was Congress that guaranteed due process hearings to be held by independent fact finders: the Administrative Law Judges.

Administrative Law Judges are assigned to all of the federal agencies to make findings of fact and issue recommended decisions to the agency head. The decisions of the Administrative Law Judges assigned to the Social Security Administration, however, are final appealable decisions. Arriving at a hearing a claimant will find that due process protections runs in both directions. The Judge essentially wears two hats, one for you and a separate one for the government.

Hat Number One: The Judge is required by law to fully develop the record and assist the unrepresented claimant in doing so. This means getting records when the claimant didn't or couldn't. This is also true if the claimant is represented by a lawyer or other representative. Sometimes, the most skilled professional representative needs or requests the assistance of the Judge in getting records. But, in the end the Judge is required to obtain all available evidence. When the Claimant is not represented the Judge must fairly question the Claimant to ensure a full and fair hearing.

Hat number two: There is another party to a Social Security Disability Hearing that is not in the Court Room. That party is the Government of the United States and the Social Security Trust Fund. The Judge has a duty to ask questions on behalf of the government because no one is there representing the government. In this sense, a Social Security Judge wears "two hats" when conducting a hearing.

When I further explained how the hearing process works unrepresented claimants appeared relaxed and confident and generally made good witnesses. At the end of the day it is your life and your disability. Who better to explain what is medically wrong with you and the effects on your life. In the final analysis you must "sell" your disability to the Judge.

If all this seems confusing don't feel too bad. One day while still in private practice I was in the Cleveland, Ohio office waiting with my client for his hearing. In came two tall, well dressed dignified looking men who turned out to be lawyers. They announced to the receptionist they were from a large firm in Cleveland, one of the best and most prestigious. Both sat down to my right and started to review their client's file. I could not help then but hear what they were saying. As they were reviewing the file I heard the youngest appearing of the two ask the older lawyer what RFC meant. The older lawyer confidently told the younger lawyer that RFC meant Recent Financial Condition. I resisted the temptation to tell them that RFC means Residual Functional Capacity, the cornerstone of the entire disability process. Sometimes even those who should know don't. Maybe these two gentlemen should have checked these easy references.

If you search www.socialsecurity.gov or www.ssa.gov you will find another link to "Disability Evaluation Under Social Security" containing what are called the Medical Listings. These categories are formally listed in the Code of Federal regulations, 20 CFR App I to Subpart P of part 404, currently found at pages 453- 594. There are 14 medical categories that Social Security has decided will result in you being found disabled if you can produce the required medical documentation. I want to point out to you here that if you meet one of the listings you may think this is good news because you will begin receiving monthly checks. In reality, in my judgment, if you receive a favorable decision based on the Medical Listings you are very ill indeed and that is not good news for you.

If you decide to go it alone, try searching: www. socialsecurity.gov or www.ssa.gov for forms and links. There you will also find the following useful.

1. Adult Disability Starter Kit with Fact Sheet and Job Worksheet,
2. What You Should Know Before You Apply for Social Security Disability Benefits, and
3. An Adult Disability Interview Sheet with Helpful Hints on How to Answer Social Security Disability Questions on several subjects.

These links do not, however, provide any help on the subject of your credibility. I will begin doing that for you starting with the next chapter.

CHAPTER 2

YOUR CREDIBILITY BEGINS IMMEDIATELY

Few issues in the Social Security disability process are more important than your credibility. You can apply online, pick up the phone or walk into your local Social Security office and an assessment of your credibility begins immediately. From that moment until the end of your case you should act like you are under oath to tell the truth at all times.

This is how I began my assessment of credibility. Once I got the computer system up and running I opened up the document that contained your very first statement on your application. I then examined every piece of evidence up to the most recent. I looked for any inconsistencies in the record. If I found a number of inconsistencies or exaggerations my index of suspicion of that person's credibility increased. Once doubt on credibility began to creep into my review it became more difficult to undo. What exactly was I looking for?

I looked for any inconsistent information you provided in writing or a statement you may have made to a Social Security employee. Did the claimant give different statements about work, medical problems, alcohol abuse, drug use and pain? I also looked for comments or observations Social Security employees made about you. When you are in the Social Security Office meeting with a staffer and you provide inconsistent statements that staff member will enter notes to that effect into your electronic file.

I further monitored my case hearing docket to see what I had scheduled. I turned on my computer and put in a scheduled claimant's social security number. Instantly the entire record was before me. The first thing I did was click on a tab called "observations". What I will find there also is what a Social Security employee noted about you or your actions when you applied in person.

A picture of that claimant began to emerge. Was there a pattern of deception or exaggeration? If so, my opinion of that claimant was being confirmed the closer the hearing date got. Was there a way the claimant could salvage his or her reputation and get me to change my view of their credibility? The answer is yes, by testimony under oath.

I don't know if a complete list on the subject of what is inconsistent and what is credible has ever been compiled. This is my attempt to provide you some guidance.

Most Judges ask questions they already know the answer to. When a Judge asks questions, they are questioning or confirming your credibility based upon inconsistencies they found in your file. Therefore, be familiar with what you have said in the past.

If your testimony on your work record is incomplete, evasive or includes prior inconsistent statements, that is a trouble sign for you. Statements about pain that are inconsistent with your anatomy are also a sign of malingering. Claiming a pain level of 10 at all times, day in, day out, no changes, no exceptions even if medicated is not the way to present your testimony.

Additionally, not knowing where, when or even the last time you worked, not remembering if you worked after your disability onset date, not remembering if you were laid off, quit or were fired or saying you were never fired when you were, forgetting the reason you were fired, having grease on your hands and saying you have not worked or can't work, being evasive about any work evaluations you had and the most damaging of all having little or no work record. Admit to part time work or work for cash if you have done it. It shows a desire to work, and that can enhance your credibility.

Your personal habits: you continue smoking when you allege you quit or are cutting back, consumption of alcohol while saying you quit or took the cure from AA, you can't remember your sobriety date, you don't know when the last time you took a "hit" or can't remember the date you got clean, you never did Crack when your records show you did and then you deny it. If you have a problem, admit it.

Living arrangements and activities of daily living (ADLS), living with others and testifying you live alone, living with family members or friends, who are on disability and you deny it, you limit your driving when you drive everywhere, telling the Judge you do nothing all day when you have young children, dogs or other animals that require your care, you have an elderly parent living with you but say you don't provide any care, you don't cook yet you live alone, you don't drive but you do get your children up, feed them and take them to school, you don't go to their games yet you have an email address that includes the title of "soccer coach mom", you tell the Judge you don't hunt or fish yet the record shows you have had a hunting license for the past 25 years, you don't go deer hunting but you go out in the woods with your gun and just sit, you don't drive yet you own a 2011 Ford F150 4 door, extended cab all tricked out, and then to top it all, you give confusing, inconsistent answers to all of these when the Judge asks.

If you drive say so. If you coach soccer do the same. If you hunt or fish come clean. You do not have to be an invalid to be disabled.

Physical and mental problems: You claim severe pain yet you aren't taking pain pills because of the side effects, you don't have the money or you are afraid of becoming hooked.

On this issue you may be asked if you self medicate or borrow pills from your spouse or mother and you are evasive. You don't have any emergency room visits for mental breakdowns yet you claim you do have mental problems. You offer testimony that you are in pain yet your doctor's notes don't mention pain at all. You have several other medical problems but your doctor doesn't have a record of you telling him about it. Why is all this so important?

When you go to your Social Security disability hearing you are asking the Judge to write you a check every month for the rest of your life. How does that fit into the credibility issue? If someone will benefit financially from their testimony then when that person testifies their credibility will be under a microscope.

When I conducted a hearing I didn't just come out and ask the claimant if they were telling the truth. My questions were directed at claimant's motivation for applying to determine if that motivation was money. Here are three questions

I usually asked younger claimants to expose their motivation.

1. "If you have never worked then how do you know that you can't work?"
2. "If I award you disability at age 24 what do you see yourself doing in the future?"
3. "If I issue you a favorable decision do you expect to be on disability the rest of your life?"

If I got an evasive answer I assumed they wanted to be on disability for the rest of their life. You must overcome the impression that you just don't want to work. This is a major credibility problem for claimants because the Social Security Administration estimates that for every favorable decision issued an average $300,000.00 is paid out over that person's lifetime. The thinking is that if you're looking for a monthly check you'll say anything to get it. Your goal should be to change this impression. Start with your testimony.

Do yourself a favor and do not try to fool the Judge. You will get caught. You are not smarter than the Judge. You are not trained in Social Security Disability like the Judge is. Don't listen to others that tell you the Judge can be fooled. Maybe you will get away with it once in awhile, but it is more likely you will not. Tell it like it is, tell the truth at all times. If you do try to fool the Judge and fail you will find an unfavorable decision in your mailbox. It is a risk not worth taking.

Next, I want to give you a few tips about how credibility works into what you put down on your application. You state you "can't do anything", "you can't walk", "you don't drive" and "you can't shower." Yet as your case develops it is clear you can walk although not very far. But you can walk, so say so. Describe what limitations you have when walking on gravel or some other uneven surface. Also, you can drive, in fact, you get in your brand new Ford F1 50 tricked out pickup truck and you drive to the Social Security field office 12 miles from your house.

You enter the office and are interviewed by a Social Security employee. The employee notes in a section of your electronic file called "observations" the following: You are neatly dressed your hair is clean, neat and combed, indicating you can bath or take a shower. The file also notes that you drove your vehicle to Social Security because you were observed through windows in the building. It is further noted that you get out of your truck without difficulty and walked into the office. Can you pick out the credibility in this paragraph? You should be able to by now. They seem like such small things. But, if you will lie about such small matters the Judge will be thinking what else will you lie about.

Remember, you do not have to be an invalid to be awarded Social Security Disability. So don't act like you are. If you drive say so but tell them how you are limited and why. Don't say you cannot walk unless you are nearly bedridden. Be candid about what you can do and can't do.

Moreover, be mindful that you are being watched and that there are people out there, even friends and neighbors that will report you to Social Security if you are applying for disability and found doing things that are inconsistent with being disabled. If you are seen mowing your lawn, carrying heavy items from to your car to the house, getting on a ladder to paint the house someone will report you. If you allege severe depression, but you are out and about all the time someone will see you. When you go to your hearing read all the statements in the file. If someone reported you it will be there. Explain it away if you can, otherwise admit it.

You should also be aware there are small one way windows in the Judge's door leading to the courtroom. The Judge can observe you through this window when you enter the hearing room.

On this one I can't speak for other Judges but this is a technique I used .

Here are some other examples of how claimants may be judged on credibility. You are generally a clean neat dresser, you don't have a lot of new clothes because you've not been working but you take pride in your appearance. On the day you go to the local Social Security office you rely on a friend's advice to go in soiled sweatpants, unshaven and dirty hair. Is this the right thing to do? Of course not, dress as well as your circumstances will allow.

Judges have performed some interesting tests to get to credibility. During one hearing a Judge was trying to get at the truth from a claimant the Judge suspected of being less than truthful. There were hints in the claimant's medical records that the claimant may have been intentionally limiting how much he could lift. The Judge reportedly attached a twenty five pound weight under the chair where the claimant sat. When the claimant testified he could only lift five pounds the

Judge asked him if he thought he could lift the chair he was sitting on. The claimant obliged and lifted the chair and the twenty five pound weight underneath. The Judge found claimant not credible and issued an unfavorable decision.

Yet another credibility issue is claimants, for whatever reason, think they have an Academy Award Winning talent and try to fake pain. You can walk with pain into the Social Security office, you can agonize as you sit down and stand up, you can moan and groan, you can complain of excruciating pain. This is all acceptable if your medical records support your symptoms and you are not exaggerating. But there is something else to consider. If you are in severe pain, the Judge will look for a history of pain medications. You can explain that you are broke and can't afford medication but if someone is really in pain, they will find a way to medicate. You may borrow some pills from your wife or friend, or self medicate. The safe bet is to disclose such practices openly, otherwise if you are in pain and not taking medication your allegations of pain will be in doubt.

And when you have an appointment at the local Social Security office or before an Administrative Law Judge, arrive early. Rather than assuming Social Security employees have little to do but to wait for your appointment the opposite is true. The Social Security Administration is swamped with disability applications and other work and if you arrive early for your appointment or hearing Social Security Administration employees will appreciate it.

I was taught early and often about the carpenter rule. To arrive early is to be on time. To arrive on time is to be late and to arrive late is to be gone. Do yourself a favor, be early, be one half hour to one hour early for your hearing. This is something positive you can do to help yourself. If the Judge gets an open spot he may ask if you are ready to go forward. If there is some issue he wants to talk with you or your representative about, you will be ready. Being early can turn into a good thing for you.

Here is an issue that can help you. The Judge can use your work record to enhance your credibility. If you have a strong and steady work history with few breaks in employment the Judge has the authority to give that great weight in deciding if you are credible.

The Judge can find support for this in a combination of a Federal regulation and a Social Security Ruling to make this finding of credibility. Think about it, a strong work record makes it unlikely you don't want to work and are in the system just to collect a check. No work record or a weak record demonstrates the opposite.

But before you set out to prove what a good worker you have been you need to decide how you are going to file your claim. There are advantages and disadvantages to each method of filing a claim that can affect your credibility.

CHAPTER 3

WHICH METHOD OF APPLYING FOR DISABILITY SHOULD I USE AND CAN IT AFFECT MY CREDIBILITY?

This short chapter presents the four ways to file for disability, the benefits and the risks of each. There are essentially four ways you can file an application for disability, they are:

1.) telephone 2.) go to the office in person 3.) file electronically or 4.) U.S. Mail. This chapter gives you the advantages and disadvantages of each method.

1. Filing an application over the telephone has the advantage that no one in the Social Security office will be able to observe you and record their impressions. Your application will, however, have notes such as you understood the questions, or that you were able to answer all questions perhaps indicating you weren't in pain. The disadvantage is if you are truly disabled you will miss an opportunity to demonstrate that on your first visit. If you file a telephone application from home you can't hand documents in and communication breaks down, such as interruption from family members.

2. Going in person to the Social Security Office has the advantage of a face to face

meeting with a Social Security employee. You can raise questions and hand documents to them, get an explanation of the process and ask follow up questions. Some of the disadvantages are: You will be carefully observed, avoid the temptation to drive to the office and to drive home when you're finished. Many claimants have their spouse drive to the Social Security office and when you're done with the meeting walk up to a truck get behind the wheel and drive off. Be consistent if you're going to have someone take you do not get behind the wheel and drive home. Another disadvantage is that employees of the local Social Security office may watch you walk into the office and upon concluding your appointment walk back out.

I've seen observations by Social Security employees stating things such as: claimant carrying his cane , claimant no longer limping , claimant walk briskly to his truck, claimant sat down and got up without difficulty, claimant did not appear to be in any discomfort.

3. Using U.S. Mail. There aren't many advantages or disadvantages that matter with this method. You can't be observed so that will not hurt your credibility and you can't be observed so that won't help either. An application by U.S. Mail is a good alternative if you can't drive, use the internet or you are hearing impaired. Although with a hearing impairment you can use a modified phone system that is available.

4. Filing the application electronically. By filing the application electronically you avoid comments like those made in the preceding paragraph. The disadvantage is that when you reach your hearing before the Administrative Law Judge you will probably be asked questions regarding your computer skills. For instance, Mr. Claimant do you have an e-mail address,

what do you send and receive through your e-mail address how many people you correspond with e-mail. Do you have a Face Book page, use twitter, pay your accounts, and conduct research. If you have a number of favorite places what are they. These questions are all designed to determine your credibility and your ability to engage in what are called activities of daily living.

The questions also test your ability in a critical area, Concentration, Pace and Persistence. What will surely follow are additional questions about your use of a computer: Your hands and fingers, reading, concentration, thinking, using a cell phone to communicate with friends and family. All of this from filing online.

You have decided to go it alone or get someone to represent you. You selected the method of filing you are most comfortable with and you file. Now Social Security tells to you wait and wait you do. But there are some steps you can take to help your case move along.

A Social Security Disability application is hard work. You have to become engaged in the process and co-operate with everyone. The next chapter tells you how you can take the first steps toward helping yourself.

CHAPTER 4

What Takes Social Security so Long, Can I get an Earlier Hearing Date and Will my Credibility be Tested

The Social Security Administration is swamped with disability applications and the horror stories have people waiting years for a hearing. What takes Social Security so long and what is it doing while you wait?

A truism about the federal government is this: there is a procedure for everything. Real progress has been made in consistently reducing the national backlog. Much of the credit is due to procedures put in place by former Social Security Commissioner Barnhart for establishing a nationwide electronic records and case processing system.

As Chief Judge of the Cleveland, Ohio Hearing Office I helped get this new system up and running. When the system was fully operational, time-consuming mailing and other hands on paperwork by staff members was drastically reduced. But first all federal employees assigned to ODAR, including Judges had be thoroughly trained to use the new equipment and software. These are not the only steps taken to keep up with the backlog.

Additional Judges have been appointed with a confirmation process that is long and difficult, in order to fill ever expanding vacancies as older Judges retire. Still, a significant backlog remains. This is due in part because as unemployment increases and our population ages so do the number of disability applications. The wait time for a hearing is being reduced nationwide but remains stubbornly long.

There are, however, steps you can take that will help. I told you in the prior chapter that pursuing a disability application is hard work. This is just the beginning. If you help Social Security employees with certain parts of their workload your case can move along. I am going to tell you how, but first understand that Social Security Offices of Disability Adjudication and Review are frequently operated differently than other offices. This requires you to keep watch for some rule changes.

I previously explained that the volume of cases is one reason for a long wait. Another is that Congress requires Social Security to help you gather all information needed for a full and fair hearing. If you provide Social Security with the documentation needed without waiting for them to get it you are helping get your case ready for hearing and speeding up the process.

When you first go into a Social Security office to file for disability have your basic identification with you, Social Security card or number, birthdates for your entire family, driver's license or other government identification. Take medical information related to your disability. If you break a leg and you have the medical records take those with you. Have all your job information organized when you go. These simple steps will help move your case along. There are other procedures that may get you an earlier hearing date. When using one of these procedures at the hearing level, the Judge assigned to your case is the one you are trying to persuade.

Here then, are your choices:

1. The Congressional Inquiry. Contact your Member of Congress. Your file

will be marked electronically with a Congressional interest flag. The Office of Disability Adjudication and Review is required to send a report to that Member of Congress on the status of your case. If the case has been assigned to a Judge, the Member of Congress will be told that and what, if any action has taken place. For example, the report might state the case is set for hearing, the Judge is reviewing the case for additional evidence needs, a hearing has been held, a decision is ready to go out, or some other status note. Generally, the Member of Congress would be told at this point if the decision is favorable but not if it is unfavorable.

Using this procedure is no guarantee that your claim will be advanced on the docket. Your case, however, does get additional attention that may ultimately move it along faster.

2. Critical Status. Critical Status can be assigned to your case when, e.g. you have documentation that the disease you suffer from has deteriorated considerably. Or you have just produced medical evidence that your original impairment may meet a Listing or are suicidal. This is truly unfortunate for you but it presents an opportunity for you to ask that your case be moved up on the Judge's docket.

Making a phone call and nothing else is not the way to get this done. Gather your medical records on this recent event together as fast as you can and get those records to Social Security. Make sure Social Security has all contact information for you and close relatives. You may have an answering machine but don't go anywhere if you don't have to. Hearing dates do open up and the worst thing that can happen is you get a call and you don't answer.

3. Dire Need. Dire need refers to severe financial difficulties and in this economy this is a frequent request. To establish Dire Need you need to submit documentation of your dire financial problems. As a Social Security Judge I wanted to see something like this: the original or a copy of an eviction notice, past due notices for rent, eviction notices, a complaint or notices of impending foreclosure on your home, dunning notices for long overdue medical bills, all with proof of your current income or lack of income. I would suggest filing a Dire Need request if you have one or more of these but if you also have overdue electric bills and heating bills, food bills or other household expenses submit those also. The more proof you submit the better your chances.

If you're represented by a lawyer or other qualified representative they will know how to file these requests on your behalf. If you're not represented by anyone the local Social Security staff or ODAR employees can assist you. If you are at the hearing level the staff person you want to contact at the hearing office is the SCT (Senior Case Tech) assigned to the Judge that has your case. Make sure you gather all your documentation first and have it ready to submit.

When the local office staff or the Judge's SCT try to reach you repeatedly and you don't answer they will wonder why. We are back to credibility. If you are claiming you are disabled you should not be out and about all the time. If the staff can't reach you after multiple tries the question becomes, where were you and what were you doing.

While you wait your file will be sent to the state agency that makes the first decision on your case. During this review Social Security may decide to send you out for an evaluation by a physician or other specialist of its choosing. When this evaluation is returned, the agency will more than likely make its first of what may be several decisions. If your own doctor's report is not yet in the file, the decision will be made without it.

When you are examined by a consulting doctor what you say or do while being examined will affect your credibility.

CHAPTER 5

What to do and not do During a Consulting Examination, How to Avoid this Credibility Trap

Social Security will send you to a doctor or other professional for a consultative exam. This person will be called an "independent" examiner. Social Security will not ask you when you can attend. You will receive a notice telling you when to go, who you will see and where. Social Security will also provide you with information on how to get reimbursed for your mileage and any legitimate food costs. In this chapter I will tell you what you need to know and what you can do to improve the outcome.

This is how it works. You filed for disability and Social Security expects you to co-operate in the development of your claim. The reason you are not contacted to see what date is best for you is that you say you are disabled, therefore, you must not be working and have no other obligations. If you are unable to attend the exam and want to change it you can by calling Social Security NOT the examiner. But be careful, however, what reason you give, remember what I have just said about you being disabled. Notes are made of your request and therefore, probably any conversation you have with an employee at Social Security. Never tell anyone at Social Security you have to check your calendar to see if the date it has given you is available. But do call and tell someone at the Social Security Office you will be at the examination as scheduled.

Be early for your appointment. Forget getting upset if the doctor is late. Do not get irritated with him or her or any of the employees in that office. Go early and wait without incident, wait hours if you have to, but if you do wait hours, report that to the Social Security Office soon after your appointment. Don't wait for your representative to suggest it. When reporting to the exam, use the suggestions in the following paragraph.

Sometimes it is the little things that count. Arrive early and make a note of the time you arrive. Note how long you wait in the reception area. Then make a note of how long you spend in the examining room waiting for someone to come in, anyone. If it is a nurse make a note of how long the nurse spends with you and then again note how long you wait alone for the doctor. Now here is the really important part. Take note of how long the doctor actually spends examining you. That is, looking into your eyes, feeling (palpating) your back or giving you a test. When you leave write it all down. If you do file a complaint your notes will support you.

The exam itself: Be courteous to everyone. But, don't get too friendly with this doctor, he is not your doctor. The doctor and staff may seem friendly and may be so. But I have seen reports where this doctor said he would help you and the written report said the opposite.

Notes will be made by the examiner of your mental status, how you walk, if you have a back complaint how easy you got on and off the examining table. Yet on your effort to get on and off the examining table, do not try to fake it. Doctors have accepted methods to check you and, yes, even trick you. You are not an actor, so don't try to be one. You will not get an academy award for your "faking" performance but you will surely lose.

There are tests the doctor can perform that will produce a result that is inconsistent with truthfulness. An example is when the doctor asks you to raise your leg back toward your head. The doctor is near your feet and you are lying on your back. You tell him that hurts when he raises your leg. The next test the doctor performs is to take one of your feet and tilt the toes back toward your head and you don't feel anything. You have been caught. This maneuver is the same as if he had raised your leg.

If you walk in with a cane the doctor is going to ask you who prescribed it. One of the worst things you can do is use a medical assistance device, a cane, walker or wheelchair that's not been prescribed for a legitimate reason. When you leave the presence of the doctor, your examination is not yet over. If you used a cane going to the exam you should use one leaving it. If a spouse or friend drove you to the doctor's office, and someone should, that person should drive you home.

Few actions can affect the doctor's opinion of you more than using a cane going into his office and walking out with it in your hand or getting into your vehicle to drive home if someone else drove to the examination.

You may be somewhat surprised when you see the report. You may even wonder if the doctor is talking about you. You find the report incomplete or unfavorable. You can overcome this by helping your own doctor help you and in turn help your credibility.

CHAPTER 6

How You Can Help Your Doctor Help You, Inconsistencies and Building on Your Credibility

A Social Security Disability application is hard work and you must keep at it. Keep legible notes and records. Keep your doctor appointments and make sure your doctor's records are complete and in good order. In this way, your doctor's records will enhance your credibility. Remember, the most important person in the Social Security disability process is you. The most important issue is your credibility.

Your doctor will take care of you on a regular basis and refer you to specialists as needed. Your family doctor is also called a primary care physician. Your family doctor directs the other doctors that are members of a team. These are consulting physicians, a specialist in one field or another.

These physicians understand that when they have completed their tests, their findings are to be sent to your primary care doctor and it is for him or her to decide what to do next in your care and treatment. This is the doctor you want on your side.

Your doctor is always busy with a lot of patients on his mind. The waiting room is full. You are told the doctor is running late and you've been sitting in the lobby waiting for your appointment. This can be frustrating. We know this is going to happen from time to time. If you prepare ahead of time you can save the doctor time and ensure there is an accurate record to support your complaints. The most important thing you can do for yourself is make certain that what you tell the doctor about your symptoms and medical issues end up in your chart. Here is an example that is instructive.

You file a disability application based in part on severe unrelenting headaches. This is a medical problem that can result in you being found disabled. It will take some persistence but it can be done. Now let's fast forward for a moment to your hearing before an Administrative Law Judge.

The Judge wants you to describe your headaches. The Judge asks, "… tell me about the severity, frequency intensity and duration of your headaches."

Going from memory you tell the Judge, "…I have these headaches, uh about 3 or 4 times a week, they last, uh about 30 minutes and when this happens I have to lie down." You testify from memory but your doctor's office notes make no mention of these episodes. There is a note in your doctor's records that you were asked to keep some kind of diary of your symptoms. You didn't keep any notes and have nothing else to say in response to the Judge's question. Your testimony is vague. You have failed to provide what the Judge is looking for, a reason to find you credible.

Compare the above example with this. You have an appointment with your primary care doctor. During this visit you complain about severe unrelenting headaches. The doctor asks you essentially the same question the Judge did about the severity, frequency, intensity and duration of these headaches. Your wife is with you at this visit so together you fill the doctor in and give very specific answers to his question. This will help because later in the process your doctor will be asked to fill out a Residual Functional Capacity form. He can fill out the form by transferring his notes or attaching a copy of his notes. This last method is not preferred by Judges. The form should be sent in completed and legible.

The doctor in his or her role as a medical quarterback orders testing with a specialist. Before leaving the doctor's office for that day's visit you simply ask your doctor if he has noted all of your complaints and symptoms. He tells you yes and you listen as he dictates into a machine. Then the doctor asks you to keep a calendar where you note the dates, severity, duration intensity and frequency of your headaches.

You get a calendar and keep your headache episodes on that calendar. Your notes look like this: wake up Monday morning at 7 A.M., 20 minutes later you have a severe headache that lasts 35 minutes, you note it is one of your most severe in days. You note that between 7 A.M. and 7:30 AM you had a headache on a scale of nine and it felt as if your head was in a vice. This lasted for 30 to 35 minutes and was so severe you put cold presses over your eyes. You further note four more of these headaches throughout the day approximately 2 hours apart. Your calendar is noted you had 15 identical episodes within 30 days.

At your next appointment your doctor asks how you are doing. You describe your last month and give him a copy of your calendar. By the time your hearing date arrives you have several months of notations. You have support for your testimony. You have the basis for a finding of credibility.

With these facts let's revisit the Judge's question. You are asked the same question. Now compare your first answer to the answer you can now provide. Your testimony is specific as to times, dates, severity, frequency, intensity and duration of your headaches. Your testimony is now supported by the detailed office notes of your personal physician. This method can make the difference between a Judge finding you credible and not credible: A Favorable decision versus an Unfavorable decision.

Claiming a disability for headaches is difficult but it is not the only difficult impairment. The Social Security Administration recognizes a disability for seizures. As a Social Security Judge is evaluating a claimant's complaint of headaches that Judge can look to the seizure literature for guidance. I suggest in presenting your headache complaints that you follow the requirements for seizures. The Listing on seizures requires proof of type, duration, intensity and frequency. As with seizures, migraine headache patients may often be alone when the headaches occur. A family member, however, can document what they observed when they saw you. Holding your head, lying down in a dark room or even crying. They should document what they saw. The first chance you get, give the note to your doctor and ask him to make it a part of your record. Just like a person with seizures would do.

Another impairment that presents difficult proof issue for claimants is back complaints. You injured your back and you are complaining of severe, excruciating pain that is causing you significant mobility problems. Doesn't it make more sense to provide a Social Security Judge with a diary of your pain and severity, duration and frequency than to wing it? And doesn't it make more sense to have some kind of diary detailing the limitations caused by your pain? Such as, you get up in the morning but are unable to straighten up. You can drive for limited amounts of time, and be specific about how long. Getting in and out of the car is the most difficult for you. But if you do drive, admit it.

You wrote down in your initial Social Security record that you can't walk but, of course, you can. On the day of your hearing you walk into the hearing room. Is this an exaggeration? Is this an area for fair inquiry? You didn't mean you couldn't walk at all when you told Social Security that. But that's not what you said. How does the

Judge know what you meant? Admit what you need to admit. On the issue of driving, I can tell you this: every Social Security Judge has heard the claimant testify he or she can only drive to the corner store. Tell the Judge how far you can drive and how often rather than saying how little you can drive. It can enhance your credibility.

Here is a different but common credibility issue often presented at a hearing. Your medical records since you were a college student reflect illicit drug and alcohol abuse. It is taking its toll on you now but you have told the Social Security Administration you are now sober for several years. When a claimant came before me and had this history my first question was: "What is your sobriety date?" For me, if a claimant didn't know his or her sobriety date, they suffered a loss of credibility. I frequently heard a claimant say in response to my request for sobriety date the following: "say what?" Or "well about three years ago."

Compare the above response with this: you walk into the hearing room and you have sign in sheets or some type of paper record from AA or other continuing sobriety program that establishes your regular attendance at meetings. Tell the Judge if you have attended meetings on a regular and consistent basis. When the Judge asks you for a sobriety date and you answer with a specific month, day and year, your answer projects pride in your accomplishment. You admit, however, that initially you went through the program before and you had a relapse for two months. But since that time and for e.g. 34 months you have been sober. Be straightforward with the Judge. Be proud of your sobriety. Based on my hearings and what other Judges have told me, it will enhance your credibility. Helping your own doctor will be all but lost, however, if you aren't careful to avoid inconsistencies in your medical record, the existence of which creates credibility issues.

Inconsistencies can be a direct reflection on your credibility. An inconsistency does not equate with credibility. If the Judge finds you or your written records have been inconsistent a number of times that can lead to a finding of not credible.

When you talk with your doctor or any doctor be consistent unless there is a good reason for a change in your medical picture. Being truthful at all times will help you be consistent. Being truthful and consistent can be supported by keeping a proper, reliable record of your pain.

CHAPTER 7

MAINTAINING A DIARY OF YOUR MEDICAL PROBLEMS AND PAIN IN A WAY THAT ENHANCES YOUR CREDIBILITY

Keeping a consistent diary of your complaints and symptoms is easy and so very important. Social Security staff and Judges are overloaded. Believe me when I tell you this, the Judges will read all of the records on a case before them but they also appreciate brevity. Make it as easy as possible on them.

Another reason to keep a diary is it helps you prepare for your hearing. It is a great reminder of symptoms you may not recall. Remember what I said about your practice testimony. Which sounds better to you my first example or the second? "Judge I don't remember the dates I had severe pain but I think this was the date." Compare that with, "Judge, I brought a calendar that shows the dates I had a 9 or 10 on the pain scale. I also have a diary which is specific about times, dates, pain type, intensity, frequency and duration.

Here is what to do. Get a paper calendar like the Christmas calendars you get in the mail. Here is an example of how you might keep a diary. You are disabled because of seizures. The Social Security regulations have a section on seizures and if you meet the requirements of each section you are disabled. The common problem with a seizure claim is that most people have seizures when no one is around. Yet one of the principle requirements of the seizure section is that typical seizures must be described.

In addition, if you are having seizures of the severity required to be found disabled, you really won't remember what happened to you once you return to normal after a seizure. This is why meeting the requirements for disability with a seizure disorder is about as difficult as it gets. If your reason for applying for disability has nothing to do with seizures don't skip this chapter. Read on. This section is to give you an example of record keeping that can be adapted to other impairments.

There is something else to keep in mind. Social Security Judges are human. Some of them continue to serve into their 80's or 90's. Some are healthy, some are not. Judges have heart attacks, diabetes, back problems and maybe even a seizure disorder. Some would be found disabled if they applied but because of the nature of the job they are able to keep working.

The Social Security Judge you appear before might even have the very same medical problem as you. But you won't know this about the Judge. Even if you have the healthiest Judge on the planet, that Judge is going to read and know the medicine and the regulations that apply to your case.

The seizure regulation requires you to describe the type or types or seizures you are having, Grand Mal, Petit Mal or both. If one type or both they each have to be documented. My experience is Grand Mal can be documented better than Petit Mal because of their very nature Grand Mal are more violent and seen by relatives more often. Your doctor will order certain studies to monitor your brain waves. If these studies are positive that is very helpful but not quite enough. The regulations require that a seizure be documented, but how? A diary, that's how.

So let's get started with an example of how to do this. Have your calendar with you or out on a table at home. If you live alone, admittedly this is going to be difficult but if you have a spouse, live with parents or have children in the house they can help you.

You may have seizures during the day, while sleeping or both. There may be someone with you when you have a seizure or you may be alone at the time of the seizure.

The "no one is around problem." This happens either at night while you are sleeping or during the day when everyone is out working. You wake up in the morning and you feel an aura about you, numb, don't know where you are or aware something happened to you. This has happened to you before. But your husband was with you. Now however, you know you urinated on yourself at night and you may have even bit your tongue because there is saliva on the pillow. Mark your calendar in this manner.

It's Tuesday morning. Mark it between Monday and Tuesday. Seizure, saliva, tongue, urine, aura or dopey. Make it your description and keep it short.

This happens at home but your wife is not there. You have a seizure and she walks in. Have her make an immediate note of what she sees. Bruised eye, blood on tongue, you don't know where you are. If someone is with you the entire time write down the approximate time it took until you are aware again.

Now you go before the Judge and he asks you to describe a typical seizure and he knows you were "out of it" during the seizure. You have a diary prepared as soon as possible after the seizure, not a day later. You give him the original (easier to read) and you keep a copy. You will have met one of the elements of the regulation, that is, to describe a typical seizure including all "phenomena."

Remember what I told you about credibility. It is going to be questioned. This is one more way to support your testimony and enhance your credibility. We have covered how to avoid conflicts in the evidence and how to document your complaints and your pain. Next comes the critical part, how to describe and prove your pain. That is, how to make it credible.

CHAPTER 8

YOU ARE IN PAIN, HOW TO DESCRIBE IT, HOW TO PROVE IT IN A WAY THAT IS CREDIBLE

O n the first day of class for Administrative Law Judges an instructor said this to us, "Everyone who appears before you will be sick, not all will be disabled." It didn't take long after I started hearing cases to realize how right he was.

Every claimant has something wrong with them ranging from severe mental disease or radically low I.Q.s to trashed backs, disabling neurological and terminal diseases to one claimant who only had a sore hip. I found some of these claimants disabled , some not.

The most common thread in all impairments is a complaint of pain of some type and at some level of frequency, intensity and duration. The problem you face then is how to distinguish your case from the lady with merely a sore hip. How do you convince the Judge your pain is real and disabling by itself or in combination with your other impairments. This chapter is not just about physical pain, because mental, emotional and even phantom pain are very real.

Mental and emotional pain can be aggravated by physical conditions which in turn can be made more intense by mental and emotional pain. In a very real sense if this describes you then you are trapped in a vicious cycle. Your physical limitations aggravate your emotional status and your emotional condition makes your physical condition worse. Physical, mental, mental, physical, around and around you go. You must, however, accurately describe it because the Judge doesn't know what you mean by pain unless you tell him. Pain is unique to each claimant. What feels like a pin prick to one person is debilitating to another.

Claimants whose testimony I found credible described their mental pain as living in a dark hole in complete despair and without any hope for a better day. They described it as feeling mentally crushed leaving them so desperate that suicide was often thought of as the only relief. This feeling in turn aggravated their physical impairments, leaving them with no energy and an increase in their physical pain requiring, in some cases, nursing home care.

These claimants further described their physical pain as searing or burning, as if someone stuck a red hot poker in their back or leg. They would describe it as aggravated by simple things such as bending over, reaching too far, too fast.

The credible claimants testified the pain radiated down one or both legs but not at the same time or at the same level of intensity. With heart attacks the chest pain was described variously as like getting hit in the chest with a sledge hammer or as if an elephant sat down on their chest.

On a pain scale of 1 to 10 with 10 representing the greatest pain, and 1 the least, credible claimants would assign a 9 on bad days and a 6 or 7 on good days. They would admit that medication helped relieve, but not erase, the pain and that it was not equally distributed. These claimants would also testify that pain medication took twenty to thirty minutes to provide relief and would, depending on the type of medication, begin to wear off after about three hours. They would describe their pain by type, intensity, frequency and duration with some corroboration from a diary, credible relative or genuine friend. Detailed medical records from a claimant's treating physician added to their credibility.

Claimant's who I found less than credible presented pain testimony that was not supported by their doctor or medical records. Testimony on the intensity of their pain exceeded that expected with an injury or disease such as theirs.

Claimants I found less than credible testified they were severely depressed, nervous, experienced frequent headaches or anxious. Yet they didn't make or keep appointments with their doctor and had no recent hospitalizations, that is, until their hearing date was scheduled. They didn't take medication because they did not want to get addicted yet the medicine prescribed would alleviate many of their symptoms. Lack of money to pay for the prescriptions was also a reason they gave for not taking legitimate medicine. Such claimants, however, always had money to pay for cigarettes and alcohol.

Claimants with physical impairments would testify about their pain in a less than convincing manner. They were vague, inconsistent or avoided my questions asking about the type, intensity, frequency and duration of their pain. They had little, if any, records to support their testimony. The records they did have were inconsistent and in some cases, even fabricated.

The claimants I found less than credible would say their pain felt like a tooth ache or a pin prick. Yet they would testify the pain was so severe they couldn't bear it. When I questioned such claimants about the pain medications they were on I would be told they were not taking any because they did not want to get addicted or didn't have the money.

Generally, I found such testimony not believable because if they were really in severe pain they would self medicate, that is, drink alcohol, smoke marijuana or borrow some meds from a friend or relative. Claimants apparently didn't understand that such an admission would enhance their credibility with me because it would emphasize how desperate they were.

Claimants that were not truthful exaggerated their symptoms and came into a hearing with canes and wheelchairs that were not prescribed by their doctor. They also testified that their pain radiated down both legs with the same level of pain at all times, that it never changed from ten, yet they drove their pickup truck to Florida in the winter time. All of this was inconsistent and therefore not credible.

The findings I made on credibility examples listed above have support in the Social Security Rulings and Regulations. When you look at pain by itself or epilepsy, chronic fatigue syndrome, headaches, migraine headaches, and other impairments there is a common issue of proof in all of them.

You can give yourself an advantage by reading the check lists, essentially, that are contained in the following regulations and rulings. They are: Social Security Ruling 87-19c, a policy interpretation of 42 U.S.C. 423(d), and credibility and Social Security Ruling 96-7p assessing credibility. SSR 96-7p.

The best way to find these is to Google them. www.google.com. A quick review of these sources will give you an advantage on what Social Security is looking for in proof of pain. The basic rule is to document your pain in terms of location, intensity, frequency and duration. Social Security recommends that a Judge look at these in a different order but it doesn't matter as long as you make it credible.

If you are worried about forgetting something, think about relating your pain this way. Just start at the top of your head. No pain there, move on down. Maybe the only pain you have is in your lower back. Take your time, don't let anyone rush you. If you misstate some of your testimony tell the Judge and correct it. Don't be timid. You have waited years for your hearing. This hearing is likely the only one you will have. Use the time wisely. Be respectful to the Judge but tell her you are nervous if you make a mistake. How to prepare for your hearing and make a credible case is next.

CHAPTER 9

How to Prepare for Your Hearing, Your Testimony and Your Credibility

You are now going to testify but you must first prepare for your hearing, a process that should have started when you first filed for disability. The next part of preparation is to co-operate at all stages of the process. If you do not co-operate for example, in the consultation process, your case may be dismissed or an unfavorable decision issued after a hearing. You can keep this from happening by staying involved.

Social Security Judges are generally a compassionate group. The law they follow comes many sources and is always changing. They work hard at the job to hold fair and full hearings. It is a good idea, therefore, not to get off to a bad start with the Judge by being late. As with all things with Social Security, be early.

I could never understand why someone would file for disability, fill out all the paperwork, gather their records, go to examinations and then wait and wait. But when their hearing date arrived ask for a continuance, call the Office of Disability Adjudication and Review (ODAR) and tell them they don't have a ride or don't show up at all.

The entire ODAR office schedule the day of your hearing is interconnected with the experts who will testify. Some experts are by phone and have a tight schedule and others go to another

Judge's hearings when your Judges daily schedule is complete. If you are late you throw a wrench in the entire day's proceedings because all of the hearings that day are dependent on the experts being ready as scheduled.

There are other reasons to be early. If you are at the hearing office ready to go early and another claimant is late you may be asked if you are ready. Your readiness helps the Judge's schedule. And if you are represented and early the Judge just might call your representative into the hearing room and resolve your case in your favor.

Here then, is my list of do's and don'ts when testifying.

1. Stand up when the Judge enters the room, and look at the Judge when answering a question. If you don't understand the question, ask the Judge to repeat it

2. Don't answer a question you don't understand or the Judge will assume you did understand the question

3. Do sit up straight in the chair if you are able to

4. Don't slouch and lean as if pain if you are not, such acting won't work

5. Do tell the Judge you can drive when you are asked, he will ask you how much and how far

6. Do be prepared to explain why you can't work any job, don't tell the Judge you can't do anything, she will decide that

7. Do tell the Judge what is the most you can do in spite of your impairments, don't tell the Judge there is absolutely nothing you can do

8. Do tell the Judge you want to work, don't give the Judge the impression you are not willing to consider anything. This is a key credibility issue

9. Do tell the Judge there are some things you can do but with limitations supported by your doctor's records, particularly your allegations of disabling pain

10. Do tell the Judge the location, duration, frequency, intensity and type of the pain you feel
    a. location, describe where or just point
    b. duration, how long it lasts
    c. frequency, that is, how often and be specific
    d. intensity, describe it on a scale of one to ten with ten being the most severe

11. Do tell the Judge you are taking medication for your pain even if you are self medicating, that is borrowing medicine from your spouse or a friend, drinking alcohol or smoking marijuana

12. Do tell the Judge if you have an alcohol problem; don't tell the Judge you are in recovery if you are not

13. If you have a relapse in alcohol treatment tell the Judge, do not deny a relapse

14. Do tell the Judge when and where specifically you had treatment, the Judge will find out anyway

15. Do know your sobriety date, don't be caught saying in response to this question: "What is your sobriety date? Say What?

16. Do describe your pain and limitations in a straight forward manner; do not exaggerate your pain

17. Do correctly and accurately describe your military record, the Judge may be a combat veteran so don't fluff your military service

18. Do dress as neat and clean as your finances allow, no identifying clothes or hats: football jerseys, religious medallions or military items

Most cases involve pain of some type so this subject comes up often. Why do claimants exaggerate symptoms? You should know that such acting will not work. All your hard work will also be wasted if you do not know anything about the one that will decide your claim, the Administrative Law Judge.

CHAPTER 10

YOUR HEARING, THE JUDGES AND YOUR CREDIBILITY

U ntil the hearing stage your case has been reviewed by doctors you have probably never met and by staff members who you certainly have never seen. You are finally going to meet the Judge that will look you right in the eye and that is a good thing for you. This book is all about credibility and its importance in the disability process. But who are the people who decide this? Where do they come from and what kind of training do they have?

It's the Administrative Law Judges (Social Security Judges), a creation of Congress. The last several years the Social Security Judge Corps has become diversified. In a prior life the corps was essentially all white male lawyers with few females and few minorities. Today, the Administrative Law Judges come from all walks of life, they are male and female, African American, Hispanic, gay and straight and every creed and color and religion.

The ALJ must be a college graduate with a law degree and arrive at the position without any serious grievances filed against them during their legal career. They must not have filed bankruptcy nor have federal liens or a criminal record. The privilege of being appointed to this position conveys the security of a well paid lifetime appointment with numerous additional benefits. It is all to make the Judges free from pressure, interference and even bribery.

To be competitive with the private sector ALJ'S receive a salary and benefit package that approaches $200,000.00. Many Judges come from the private practice of law while still others are promoted from within the federal government or from state legal and judicial positions. Still others come from the ranks of the military and J.A.G. Officers. The Judge selected to hear your case is therefore well-educated well-trained and well paid, specializing in Social Security cases with the goal of disposing 500 to 700 cases per year. Social Security Judges are the only Administrative Law Judges who issue final decisions. Administrative Law Judges assigned to the other federal agencies issue recommended decisions. All of this ensures that Administrative Law Judges independence from interference or pressure from superiors is guaranteed.

You can, of course, rehearse your presentation for your hearing but that could lead to overstating your case. I recommend you become very familiar with your medical records and medical evidence and how you're going to describe their effect on your daily life. You are the one living with a disability and only you can describe the profound impact it has on you. Only you can accurately describe the level of pain and the intensity, frequency and duration of that pain. You don't, however, want to memorize your testimony because the judge is going to ask you questions you didn't expect. Rehearsing the answers won't help you. Knowing your medical record and being prepared to describe your pain will.

Many of the questions I asked I already knew the answers to from the record. Memorization wouldn't help in this instance. My best advice is to listen to the Judge's question and answer that question. The Judges are very busy, each Judge holds between 500 to 700 hearings a year and reviews a great many more. So answering a question directly becomes important.

The Judge will ask you questions based upon the five step process of disability. Credibility is the foundation of the process. A credibility fact finding hearing will be the basis for the Judge's decision. A Judge's decision will weave its way through the five step process to a conclusion of favorable or unfavorable reflecting her opinion of your credibility.

But before your hearing begins there is an important decision you will have to make. You are entitled to a face to face hearing with your Judge. The alternative is two types of video hearings. One is a video with you and your representative in one location and the Judge in another, usually his or her regular ODAR office. You and your representative will be in what is called a remote site. This will be a secure site in a government owned or rented space. My last office where I held hearings was the Seven Fields Office. We had a remote site in the Federal Courthouse in Erie, Pennsylvania. I stayed in Seven Fields and the claimant was in Erie. The video connected us, I could see them and they could see me.

The second type of video has the Judge in his or her usual setting but this time the claimant and his representative are in the representative's office with a pre approved set of video equipment. You, as a claimant can assert your right to a face to face hearing in person and avoid all types of video hearings.

You probably won't know you are scheduled for a video hearing until you receive your hearing notice and therefore won't be able to object to it beforehand. Now your dilemma is this. If you ask for a face to face hearing your case has to be continued until the Judge has a schedule of such cases. Do you then, ask for a face to face hearing and in the process have your case continued or do you stay with the video hearing. How much of an additional wait is up to each individual Judge.

The decision to ask for a face to face hearing is yours as a claimant. In reality, those of you who are represented will be asked by your representative to reject the video hearing. Most Judges understand this and are aware of the lawyers that always have their clients reject a video hearing.

Here are some of the issues to consider when asking for a face to face hearing. The video equipment owned and operated by Social Security produces a clear picture on your end and on the Judges end. I found, however, there is no substitute for a hearing in person. You have waited all this time and hopefully invested a great deal of work to get ready and then you agree to do it by video. If you do that, you will waste a great opportunity to present your case face to face.

Assuming you get by the issue that your case will be continued if you ask for a face to face hearing you want to ask yourself what is the down side to a person to person hearing. If you have an alcohol addiction the Judge will notice that as soon as you enter the room. The Judge will observe your eyes, the color of your face and smell alcohol. He will be able to see anything wrong with you that can seen clearly by a face to face hearing in a small courtroom.

If there is something you want to show the Judge you will be able to do that, such as a brace, a deformity or something that would benefit you if the Judge could see it up front and close. The Judge will be able to hear you better and the chances of any miscommunication are diminished. Most important in my view is the Judge will be able to get a feel for your disability, that close feeling you can only demonstrate if you are actually in the room. You or your counsel will be able to hand the Judge new evidence.

In a video hearing you will be more distant from the Judge than face to face. The Judge has the ability to zoom in on you but that is no substitute for being in the room. The audio may be challenging and you cannot hand the Judge any recent exhibits through a video hookup. The document can be faxed to the Judge in the hearing room but the delay can be frustrating to a Judge who wants to move matters along.

There is an additional problem with the video held in your lawyer's office with you in your lawyer's office. The lawyers have to get approval of the type of equipment used. There are few regulations as to how the office setup is organized. The lighting can be poor and I found myself always asking the claimant to repeat what she said.

The nature of the video from your lawyer's office is such that the hearing times for that day are provided a block of time by Social Security due to a feed from your office through Social Security to the Judge's office. There are technical problems of disconnection and the most annoying to me, when the assigned block of time expires, middle of a hearing or not, you are dropped. It should be clear that I favor face to face hearings. But if the distance is prohibitive and the weather doesn't co-operate then the video hearing looks like a smart move.

You have made your decision on the type of hearing you will have, you have a basic understanding of how the hearing is conducted and the Judges selected. And you should know by now that the Judge will be examining your credibility. But, your hearing notice also said there would be an expert or two in the hearing room. You should know if they will Judge your credibility also, the subject of Chapter 11.

EXPERTS AT YOUR HEARING, ARE THEY ALSO GOING TO JUDGE MY CREDIBILITY?

Credibility is important because it is a finding that can best be left to the Judge who hears your case and sees you testify.

The experts at your hearing may (if they are present) also see and hear your testimony but any opinion they form of your credibility must keep to themselves. This is the hearing Judge's decision, one that is "reserved to the Commissioner." This means the Commissioner of Social Security.

This chapter will take you through the experts at your hearing. There can be two such experts and sometimes they're both at the hearing. They can appear in person or by the telephone. They are a Medical Advisor and a Vocational Expert. The testimony of the Medical Advisor is based on your record. Watching and listening to you testify in person is not required.

The Medical Advisor can be a specialist in the area that includes your impairment. Or he/she can be a generalist that is qualified to testify on your medical issues. If your case involves a psychiatrist's specialty then in that event the medical advisor will be in that field. Occasionally, a psychologist will be used if an M.D. is unavailable. On child's cases (not a subject of this book) the medical advisor will be a pediatrician or a doctor that has seen young adults and followed them from childhood.

The first question I asked the Medical advisor is the level of exertion you are able to perform or that you are limited to. This is your Residual Functional Capacity or RFC. What is the most you can do in spite of your medical impairments. The doctor's answer puts you in an exertional category, heavy, medium, light or sedentary. If the doctor says yes to any one of the next two questions, you will likely be found disabled.

"Doctor, are you familiar with the Medical Listings for adults." And a few other introductory questions preferred by each Judge. "Doctor, do you have an opinion to a reasonable degree of medical probability whether the claimant's impairments meets any of the listings." If the doctor says yes then he/she must give medical reasons from your records.

If the Medical Advisor's answer is no to the first question, then the Judge will move onto the second question. "Doctor, do you have an opinion to a reasonable degree of medical probability whether the claimant has one or more impairments the combination of which would equals the listings." Some Judges leave out the combination portion and simply ask if the impairments equal the listings.

A Judge can decide that your impairments meet the listings ahead of or at the time of the hearing. The Judge cannot decide your case on an equals the listings basis without a doctor's testimony or doctor's opinion. As with all things in the law, there are exceptions to this brief explanation of the role of the medical advisor. The Judge can also reject the doctor's answer be it favorable or unfavorable.

Moreover, the Judge is the decider of all facts in the record. This includes your medical record and whether it supports the doctor's testimony. This is again called "reserved to the Commissioner." The Medical Advisor provides a medical opinion that may or may not be accepted by the Judge. The doctor may or may not believe your testimony but he may not say so. The issue of whether or not your testimony is credible is "reserved to the Commissioner."

The Vocational Expert is one who is prequalified by the Social Security Administration to give testimony on vocational, that is, job issues. The Vocational Expert, like the Medical Advisor, can testify by telephone so like the Medical Advisor, does not have to be present. This then is an important difference. The Vocational Expert will answer questions from the Judge that are hypothetical and the answers the Vocational Expert gives will be about a hypothetical person, not you individually. Remember I told you above that you will have to work hard and there are a lot of forms to fill out? And remember I told you to fill them in as much detail as possible?

This is where it all comes together. The Vocational Expert's testimony that there are jobs for an individual like you in the national or regional economy in significant numbers is based in large part on the forms you fill out.

The Judge will ask if there any jobs in the national or regional economy in significant numbers for an Individual such as you that can lift, carry, stand, walk, climb, push, pull and perform other functions. The Vocational Expert will give the Judge a number of jobs you have never heard of. And the Judge will decide if the answers you put on the forms and your testimony are credible and then work that into your decision.

The purpose of this chapter has been to explain the role of the experts. I assure you that neither a Medical Advisor nor a Vocation Expert may venture an opinion on your credibility. Nor may they offer observations of what they saw in a parking lot or in the waiting room of the hearing office that are not a made a part of the record. This type of offering is most often made in attempt to prejudice the Judge. If you hear such a comment you must strongly object to it. The Judge will recognize that a fair hearing issue is being raised.

CONCLUSION

I spent 33 satisfying years in the private practice of law representing Social Security Disability clients. They came to me after years of toiling in the factories and industry of Northeast Ohio.

Men and women showing the wear and tear from 30 to 40 years of back breaking work. They learned to adjust as their physical and mental condition deteriorated. Eventually, however, the strength and stamina required to do the work was too much for them and they could not continue. The employers could no longer keep them employed because these employees could not sustain the work load, 8 hours a day, 5 days a week in the competitive work force.

For 33 years I represented these good people and they rewarded me with a decent living for my own family. But, they gave me something far more important than a decent living. They gave me their trust and their friendship. They shared their hopes and dreams. They told me of their faith in government's ability to provide due process hearings to evaluate their disability.

While I served as an Administrative Law Judge, claimants came before me eager to tell their life's story and explain why they couldn't work. Willing to work, they would testify, but unable to. To their credit they also came to tell me the truth. And those that came to tell the truth were winners in many ways. They held their heads high and retained their dignity, and were found to be entirely credible.

The subject matter of this book is not easily grasped by professionals let alone claimants not intimately familiar with the Social Security system. If you follow the advice in this book and be truthful at all times you be glad you did.

R.A.M.

ABOUT THE AUTHOR

Ronald A. Marks, Esq.

Judge Marks graduated from Youngstown State University, The Ohio Northern University College of Law and attended the University of Wisconsin. Judge Marks is published in The Ohio State University Law Review, The Ohio Northern University Law Review, The Ohio Northern University College of Law Writ and The Practical Lawyer.

Judge Marks represented Social Security disability clients for 33 years in the private practice of law and in 2004 was appointed a U. S. Administrative

Law Judge assigned to the Cleveland, Ohio Social Security Disability Hearing Office.

Judge Marks served as Chief Judge for the Cleveland Hearing Office and in March 2008 he transferred to the Seven Fields Hearing Office in Pennsylvania where he remained until June 1, 2010. On that date he began serving as Judge of the Social Security Disability Appeals Council/ Decision Review Board, a position he held until his retirement on October 31, 2010.

Judge Marks resides near Youngstown, Ohio where he continues to lecture, write and con-sult with law firms and national corporations on Social Security disability issues.

Made in the USA
San Bernardino, CA
26 November 2014